WEEKLY WR READER

EARLY LEARNING LIBRARY

Let's Read About Dinosaurs

Stegosaurus

by Joanne Mattern
Illustrations by Jeffrey Magniat

Reading consultant: Susan Nations, M.Ed., author/literacy coach/ consultant in literacy development

Science consultant: Philip J. Currie, Ph.D., Professor and Canada Research Chair of Dinosaur Palaeobiology at the University of Alberta, Canada

Please visit our web site at: www.garethstevens.com
For a free color catalog describing Weekly Reader® Early Learning Library's
list of high-quality books, call 1-800-542-2595 (USA) or 1-800-387-3178 (Canada).
Gareth Stevens Publishing's fax: (877) 542-2596

Library of Congress Cataloging-in-Publication Data

Mattern, Joanne, 1963-
    Stegosaurus / by Joanne Mattern.
       p. cm. — (Let's read about dinosaurs)
    Includes bibliographical references and index.
    ISBN-10: 0-8368-7697-0 ISBN-13: 978-0-8368-7697-0 (lib. bdg.)
    ISBN-10: 0-8368-7704-7 ISBN-13: 978-0-8368-7704-5 (softcover)
    1. Stegosaurus—Juvenile literature. I. Title.
 QE862.O65M25   2007
 567.915'3—dc22   2006029988

This edition first published in 2007 by
Weekly Reader® Early Learning Library
An Imprint of Gareth Stevens Publishing
1 Reader's Digest Rd.
Pleasantville, NY 10570-7000 USA

Managing editor: Valerie J. Weber
Art direction, cover and layout design: Tammy West

Printed in the United States of America

2 3 4 5 6 7 8 9 10 10 09 08 07

Note to Educators and Parents

Reading is such an exciting adventure for young children! They are beginning to integrate their oral language skills with written language. To encourage children along the path to early literacy, books must be colorful, engaging, and interesting; they should invite the young reader to explore both the print and the pictures.

Let's Read about Dinosaurs is a new series designed to help children read about some of their favorite — and most fearsome — animals. In each book, young readers will learn how each dinosaur survived so long ago.

Each book is specially designed to support the young reader in the reading process. The familiar topics are appealing to young children and invite them to read — and re-read — again and again. The full-color photographs and enhanced text further support the student during the reading process.

In addition to serving as wonderful picture books in schools, libraries, homes, and other places where children learn to love reading, these books are specifically intended to be read within an instructional guided reading group. This small group setting allows beginning readers to work with a fluent adult model as they make meaning from the text. After children develop fluency with the text and content, the book can be read independently. Children and adults alike will find these books supportive, engaging, and fun!

— Susan Nations, M.Ed., author, literacy coach,
and consultant in literacy development

Who is this big dinosaur?
Its name is Stegosaurus
(steh-guh-SORE-us).
What is on his back?
Let's find out!

Two rows of flat **plates** lined Stegosaurus's back and tail. These plates were made of bone.

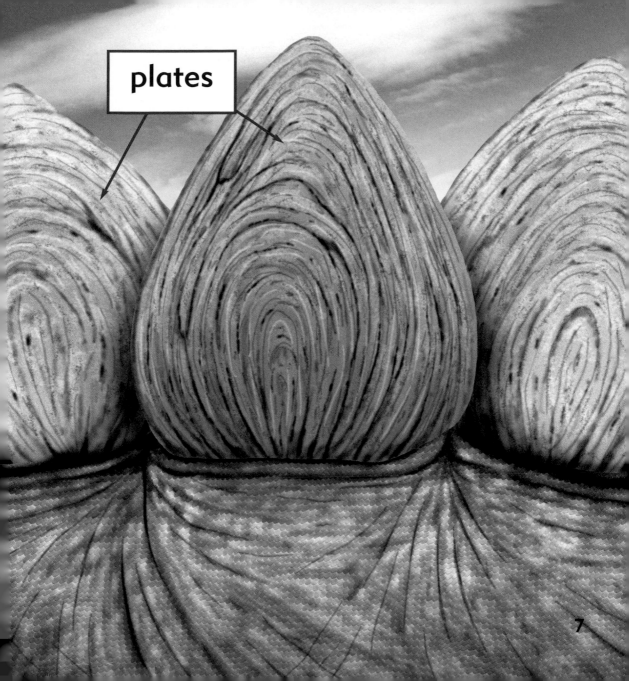

plates

The plates on Stegosaurus's back helped it stay warm. They soaked up heat from the Sun to warm the dinosaur.

Stegosaurus was about the size of a bus. It weighed as much as two cars.

11

Stegosaurus had a long, heavy tail. Spikes poked out at the end. This dinosaur's tail was a powerful **weapon**! It could swing its tail and hurt other dinosaurs.

Stegosaurus's head was about the same size as a horse's head. Its brain was the same size as a person's fist! Its brain was small for such a big body.

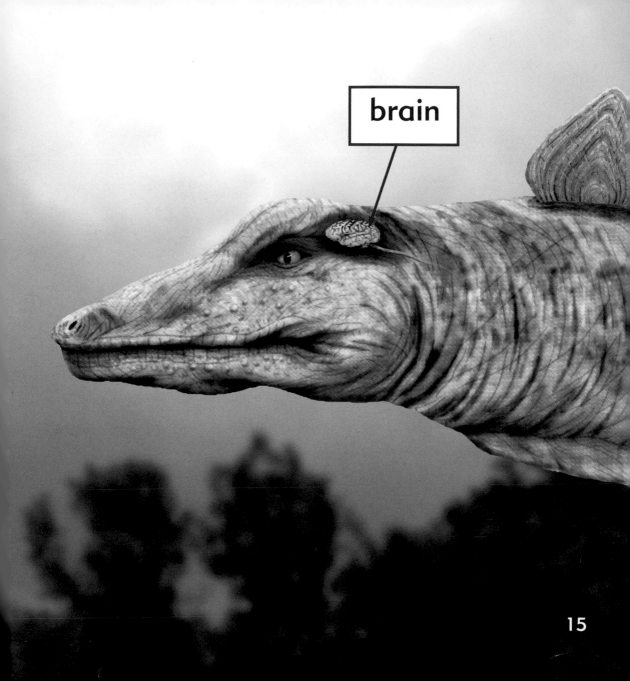

brain

Stegosaurus ate plants. Large **herds** traveled together while they ate.

Stegosaurus laid eggs. In time, each egg **hatched**. The baby dinosaurs could take care of themselves as soon as they were born.

Stegosaurus died out a very long time ago. In 1876, a scientist found some Stegosaurus **fossils**. Today we can see Stegosaurus bones in museums.

Glossary

fossils — bones or remains of animals and plants that died a long time ago

hatched — came out of an egg

herds — large groups of animals

museums — places where interesting objects are shown to the public

plates — flat pieces of bone

scientist — someone who studies nature

weapon — something that can be used in a fight

Books

A *Busy Day for Stegosaurus*. Smithsonian's Prehistoric Pals (series). Dawn Bentley (Soundprints)

Dinosaur Profiles: Stegosaurus. Andrea Due (Thomson Gale)

Stegosaurus. Dinosaurs (series). Michael P. Goecke (Buddy Books)

Stegosaurus. Discovering Dinosaurs (series). Daniel Cohen (Bridgestone Books)

Web Site

Stegosaurus Fact Sheet

www.enchantedlearning.com/subjects/dinosaurs/facts/Stegosaurus
This Web site has lots of fun facts about Stegosaurus plus drawings of the dinosaur too.

Publisher's note to educators and parents: Our editors have carefully reviewed this Web site to ensure that it is suitable for children. Many Web sites change frequently, however, and we cannot guarantee that a site's future contents will continue to meet our high standards of quality and educational value. Be advised that children should be closely supervised whenever they access the Internet.

Index

About the Author

Joanne Mattern has written more than 150 books for children. She has written about weird animals, sports, world cities, dinosaurs, and many other subjects. Joanne also works in her local library. She lives in New York State with her husband, three daughters, and assorted pets. She enjoys animals, music, going to baseball games, reading, and visiting schools to talk about her books.